# REAL WORLD DATA

# GRAPHING TRANSPORT

Deborah Underwood

Heinemann

**www.heinemann.co.uk/library**
Visit our website to find out more information about **Heinemann Library** books.

To order:
☎ Phone 44 (0) 1865 888066
▤ Send a fax to 44 (0) 1865 314091
▢ Visit the Heinemann Bookshop at www.heinemann.co.uk/library to browse our catalogue and order online.

Heinemann Library is an imprint of Pearson Education Limited, a company incorporated in England and Wales having its registered office at Edinburgh Gate, Harlow, Essex, CM20 2JE – Registered company number: 00872828
Heinemann Library is a registered trademark of Pearson Education Limited
Text © Pearson Education Ltd 2009
First published in hardback in 2009
First published in paperback in 2009
The moral rights of the proprietor have been asserted.

Edited by Nancy Dickmann, Rachel Howells, and Sian Smith
Designed by Victoria Bevan and Geoff Ward
Illustrated by Geoff Ward
Picture Research by Mica Brancic and Elaine Willis
Originated by Modern Age
Printed and bound in China by Leo Paper Group

13-digit ISBN 978 0 431 02949 8 (hardback)
13 12 11 10 09
10 9 8 7 6 5 4 3 2 1

13-digit ISBN 978 0 431 02963 4 (paperback)
13 12 11 10 09
10 9 8 7 6 5 4 3 2 1

**British Library Cataloguing in Publication Data**
Underwood, Deborah
   Graphing transport. - (Real world data)
   388'.0728

A full catalogue record for this book is available from the British Library.

**Acknowledgements**
The publishers would like to thank the following for permission to reproduce photographs:
© Alamy pp.**8** (Sean Sprague), **10** (Graham Harrison), **25** (Jim West); © Corbis pp.**4** (Jon Hicks), **6** (Frans Lanting), **13** (epa, Gerry Penny), **14** (epa, Wolfgang Kumm), **17** (epa, Michael Reynolds), **20** (Nik Wheeler), **22** (Stephanie Maze), **27** (SYGMA); © Getty Images (Justin Sullivan) p.**19**

Cover photograph of a train, reproduced with permission of ©Getty Images (Photographer's Choice).

Every effort has been made to contact copyright holders of any material reproduced in this book. Any omissions will be rectified in subsequent printings if notice is given to the publishers.

The publishers would like to thank Harold Pratt for his assistance in the preparation of this book.

# CONTENTS

Some words are printed in bold, **like this**. You can find out what they mean by looking in the glossary, on page 30.

A bicycle carries a girl along the grassy path leading to her school. A lorry full of fresh vegetables travels from a farm to a grocery shop. The space shuttle zooms high above the Earth, carrying people and supplies to the space station. The bicycle, the lorry, and the space shuttle are all types of **transportation**. They move people and **goods** from one place to another.

Today people can travel through the air, over the land, and across the oceans. A hang-glider, a horse-drawn cart, a canoe, a helicopter, a moving van, and a cruise ship are just a few of the many types of transportation.

Different types of transportation are good for different things. A school bus would not be very helpful if you needed to cross an ocean. A jet plane would get you to school quickly, but you might have trouble finding a place to land! Some types of transportation, such as walking and cycling, use only muscle power. Others are powered by **fuels** such as petrol or diesel. A type of transportation common in one country may be rare in another.

Trams and double-decker buses are two of the types of transportation used in Hong Kong.

# Transport tables

To learn more about transportation, we can compare many types of information, or **data**. To organize the data, we can write it down in tables. This table gives common speeds for some types of transportation.

| Method | Speed (miles per hour) |
|---|---|
| Walking | 3 |
| Cycling | 15 |
| Driving car in town | 25 |
| Driving car on highway/motorway | 65 |

# Charts and graphs

Sometimes information is easier to understand when we see it in charts or graphs. Charts and graphs make it easy to compare one piece of information with another. They also help us see patterns in the data. This bar chart uses bars to show the same data as the table. The taller the bar, the faster the kind of transportation it represents.

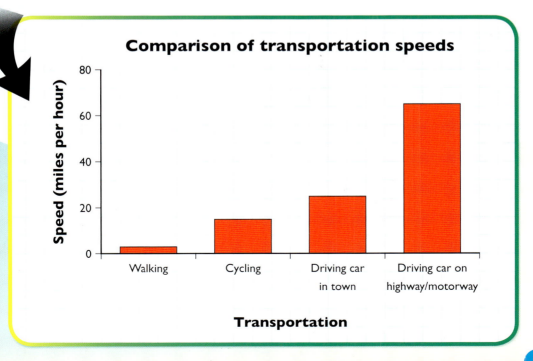

**Comparison of transportation speeds**

# PEOPLE POWER

Two important types of **transportation** use muscles, not motors. All over the world, people walk and ride bicycles to get around.

Walking is the main form of transportation in many places. Some people walk because they do not have cars or bikes. Others walk to get exercise. In African countries south of the Sahara desert, about half of all trips are made by walking.

Cycling is also a common way to get around. Bicycles cost less than cars. Cyclists can move faster than people on foot. Like walking, cycling is good exercise. People who cycle instead of drive help reduce traffic on streets. They also help reduce **pollution** in the air.

In Davis, California, USA, about 15 percent of people cycle to work. Davis is flat, so cycling is easy there. Eighty-four kilometres (fifty-two miles) of off-road cycle paths mean cyclists do not have to ride on streets full of cars. Bikes are also popular in the Netherlands, where people use bikes for about 25 percent of their journeys.

 These women from Madagascar carry wood on their heads. Walkers sometimes use wheelbarrows or carts to help them carry more.

## Cycling with power

Electric bikes, or e-bikes, have become popular in China. Some of these bikes have pedals and motors. Others are more like scooters. They are faster than regular bikes, and are allowed in bike lanes in cities. There may be over 40 million of them on the streets of China today.

## Pie charts

Pie charts show the percentages that make up a whole. These pie charts show the ways people get around in two cities: London, UK and Dakar, Senegal. A **key** shows which colour represents which type of transportation. Dakar's walking slice is much bigger, because more people there walk to get around. London's **public transport** slice is bigger, because more people in London use public transport.

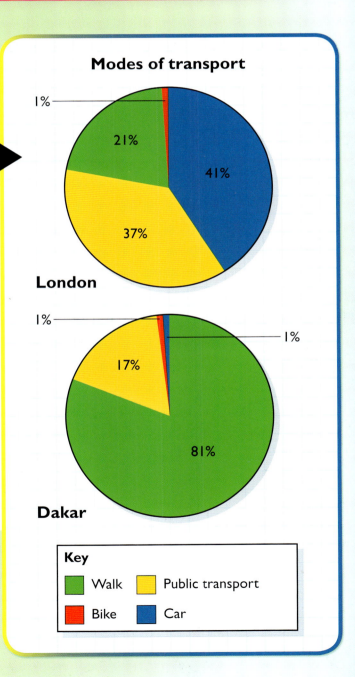

### Modes of transport

London

1%
21%
41%
37%

Dakar

1%
1%
17%
81%

**Key**

- Walk
- Public transport
- Bike
- Car

# ANIMAL ASSISTANCE

Before cars and aeroplanes, how did people carry loads from one place to another? One way was by using animals to help them. For example, Pony Express riders and their horses once carried bags of mail between the states of Missouri and California in the United States, a distance of nearly 3,200 kilometres (2,000 miles). Animals may be used to carry people and supplies. They can also be used to pull carts, wagons, or sleds.

Animals are still used as **transportation** in many parts of the world. Camels carry salt and other supplies across the Sahara desert. African traders use oxcarts to carry their fruit and vegetables to market. During Alaska's Iditarod race, teams of dogs pull sleds through 1,850 kilometres (1,150 miles) of snow and ice.

 Some people in Pakistani villages use oxcarts as transportation.

# Animal pros and cons

Some animals, such as horses, move more quickly than humans. Others, such as oxen, move slowly but can carry heavy loads. Animals can travel in some places cars can't. For example, mules in the Grand Canyon National Park, USA, carry tourists down steep, zig-zagging trails.

Animal transportation also has disadvantages. Animals require food, water, and other care. They may be difficult to train. Some people believe that humans do not have the right to make animals pull carts or carry riders.

## Heavy loads

Without labels, graphs do not make any sense. This graph shows the weight that different animals can pull or carry. The labels on the **y-axis** (the vertical line on the left side of the graph) show the number of kilograms that can be carried by each form of transportation. The labels on the **x-axis** (the horizontal line along the bottom of the graph) show what type of transportation each bar stands for.

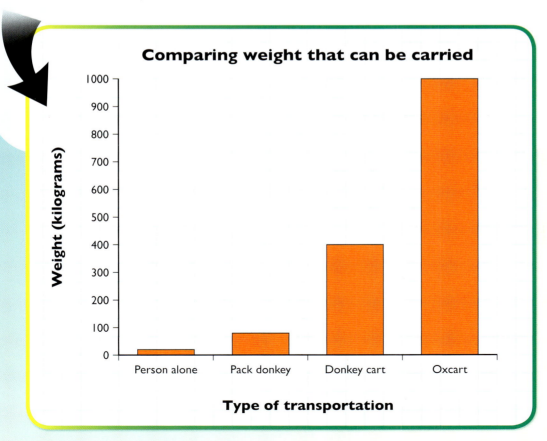

**Comparing weight that can be carried**

Weight (kilograms) — Person alone, Pack donkey, Donkey cart, Oxcart

**Type of transportation**

# TRAIN TRAVEL

Trains are vehicles that move over rails or tracks. Often the tracks are two steel rails. The first trains carried a supply of water, and coal or wood for **fuel**. Burning the fuel heated the water and made steam. The steam powered the train and made the wheels turn. Now most trains run on diesel fuel or electricity.

In places such as Europe and Japan, passenger trains are a popular type of **transportation**. In the United Kingdom many people use commuter trains to get to and from work. In the United States passenger trains were an important form of transportation in the late 1800s and early 1900s. Their use began to decrease in the 1920s as cars became popular.

However, many trains still carry **goods** in the United States, as well as in other places around the world.

## High-speed trains

High-speed trains can travel much faster than traditional trains. The train speed record of 361 miles (581 kilometres) per hour was set in 2003 by a Japanese **maglev** train. Maglev trains work differently than normal trains. When wheels rub against train tracks, it slows trains down. Strong magnets lift maglev trains a small distance above the tracks. This lets them travel faster. The magnets also move the trains forward.

The Eurostar high-speed train travels in a tunnel beneath the English Channel. It whisks passengers from London to Paris in just two hours and fifteen minutes.

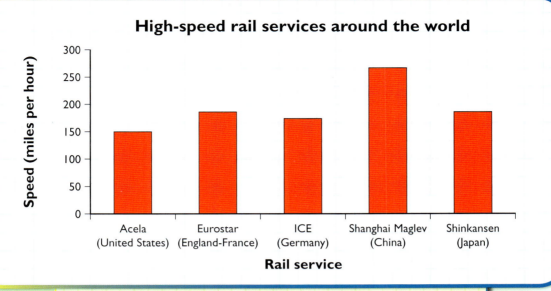

High-speed rail services around the world

 This bar chart shows the speeds of some of the high-speed rail services around the world.

# Line graphs

Line graphs show how one thing affects another. They are often used to show how something changes over time. Time is usually shown on the **x-axis**. Between the years 1840 and 2000, the number of kilometres of railway track used in the United States rose, then fell.

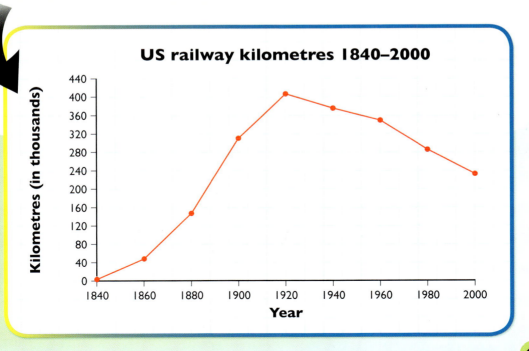

US railway kilometres 1840–2000

# SAILING SHIPS

In the days before aeroplanes, crossing the sea meant long, and sometimes dangerous, journeys aboard ships. A ship called the *Mayflower* took settlers from the United Kingdom to the United States in 1620. It took over two months to cross the Atlantic Ocean. Even today, a cruise across the Atlantic takes six days. You could fly the same distance in seven hours.

But ships are still an important means of **transportation**. They travel the world's oceans, rivers, lakes, and other bodies of water. Ships are slower than aeroplanes, but are a much less expensive way to carry **cargo** between countries, or from one part of a country to another.

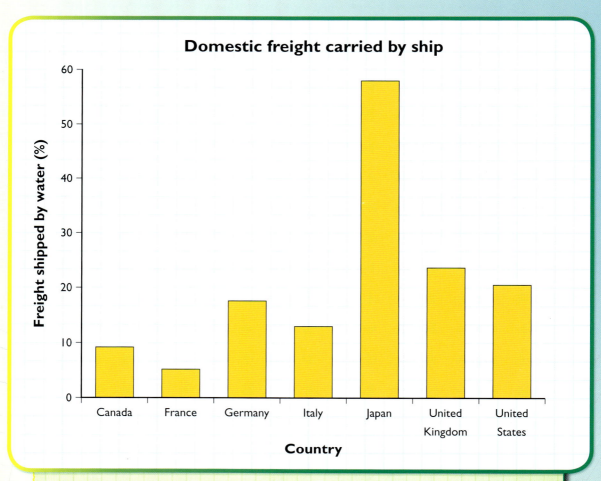

 This bar chart shows how much **domestic freight** was carried by ship in each place. Japan is surrounded by water, so most shipments within Japan were made by boat.

# Types of ships

There are many types of ships sailing the seas. Container ships carry **goods** in large boxes called containers. After its journey aboard ship, a container can be loaded directly onto a train or a lorry to continue its trip. The largest container ship can carry 11,000 of these containers.

Bulk carriers transport unpackaged things such as iron ore and coal. Tankers move liquids and gases (such as oil and chemicals) across the seas. Other ships carry general cargo. Fishing boats catch fish for people to eat.

Ships do still carry passengers, too. People take holidays on cruise ships, which are like floating hotels. They have restaurants, swimming pools, and even theatres. Many waterfront cities are served by boats called ferries. They carry people and sometimes their cars from one place to another.

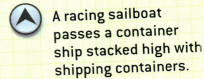 A racing sailboat passes a container ship stacked high with shipping containers.

**World fishing fleet vessels**

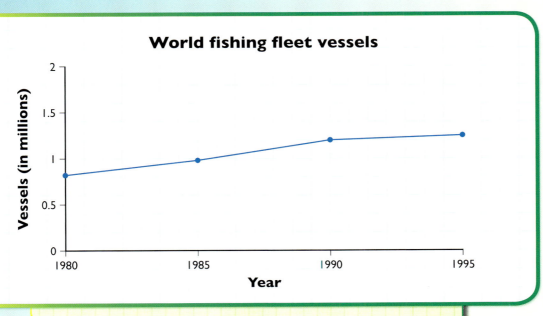

 This line graph shows the increase in number of the world's fishing boats over a 15-year period.

The invention of the aeroplane changed the way the world travels. The Wright Brothers built the first aeroplane. During its 1903 flight, it carried one person. The plane was in the air for 12 seconds, and flew only about 3 metres (10 feet) off the ground.

Today, an Airbus A380 aeroplane carries 555 passengers. It can travel a distance of 15,200 kilometres (9,450 miles) and can fly at speeds up to 1,090 kilometres (677 miles) per hour.

## Plane power

Aeroplanes cross oceans and mountains easily. Because they are fast, they carry letters and other **cargo** that needs to be moved quickly. However, it costs more to carry things by air than by rail or ship.

A **fuel** made from oil powers most aeroplane engines. The engines move the plane forward. The wings are shaped so that air flowing around them makes the plane rise into the air.

### Plane v. helicopter

Unlike aeroplanes, helicopters can take off straight up into the air. Planes must move forward to stay aloft, but helicopters can hover in the air. This means they can be used in ways aeroplanes can't – for instance, to rescue people stranded by floods. In 2005, a helicopter landed on the snowy peak of Mount Everest, the world's tallest mountain.

An Airbus A380 aeroplane is longer than three tennis courts placed end to end.

# Labels and scales

This line graph shows the increase in the number of passengers in United Kingdom airports. The **x-axis** is labelled "Year". The **y-axis** is labelled "Airport Passengers". The y-axis label here also gives the **scale** of the graph. The scale says the numbers are given in millions. This means that in 1965 there were 20 million passengers, not just 20. The bar chart below the line graph compares passengers in the top airports around the world.

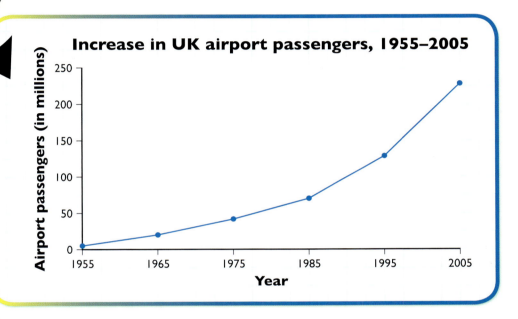

**Increase in UK airport passengers, 1955–2005**

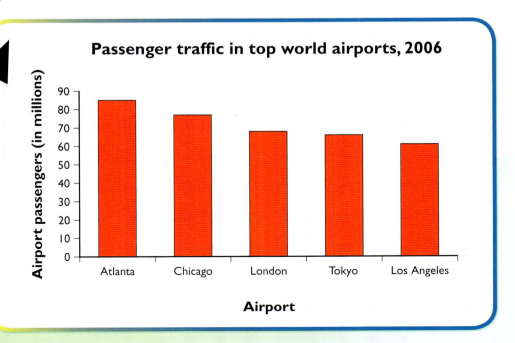

**Passenger traffic in top world airports, 2006**

# CAR CRAZY

Motor vehicles such as cars, lorries, and sport utility vehicles have completely changed the way many people travel. Around the world, the use of motor vehicles is growing. Unfortunately, motor vehicles cause problems. They make **pollution**. Most also run on **fuels** made from oil, and the Earth has a limited amount of oil.

People in North America and Europe use motor vehicles a lot. In the United Kingdom, there were 572 motor vehicles for every 1,000 people in the year 2005. In the same year, there were 804 motor vehicles for every 1,000 people in the United States.

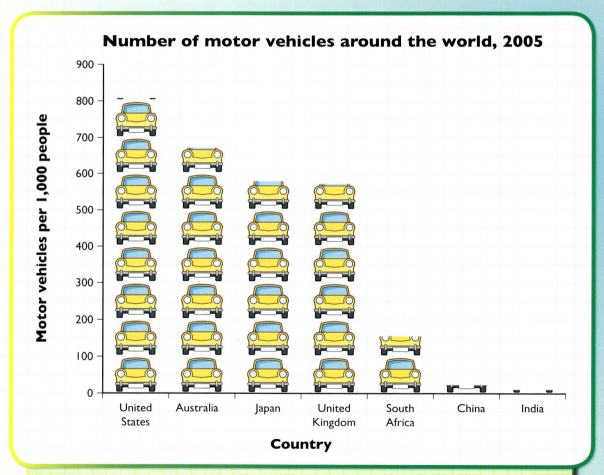

Number of motor vehicles around the world, 2005

 A pictogram uses pictures to show **data**. This pictogram shows the number of motor vehicles for every 1,000 people in a country. Each picture of a car means 100 actual vehicles.

# Car use climbs

In the past, car use was not nearly as common in most parts of Asia, Africa, and South America. But now car use is growing sharply in places such as China and India. In 2001–2002, about 510,000 cars were sold in India. Five years later, over one million were sold. China made five times as many cars in 2005 as it did in 2000.

What is causing this increase? These countries have changed in a way that means more people have money to spend on cars. And just as in other countries, some people feel that owning a car will make others respect them more. Both countries are spending lots of money to improve their roads. This makes owning a car even more attractive.

 This picture of Beijing, China, shows one of the problems caused by a rise in car ownership: more traffic jams.

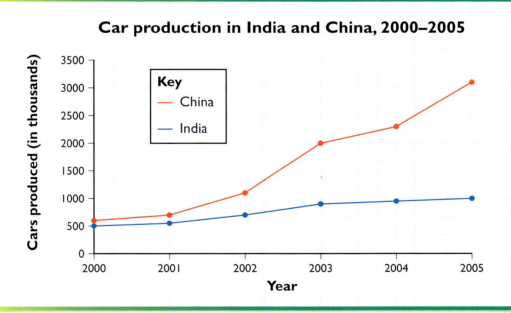

**Car production in India and China, 2000–2005**

Key
— China
— India

Cars produced (in thousands) / Year

 Car use is increasing in China and India. Car production is increasing in both countries, too. This double line graph shows the big jump in car production between the years 2000 and 2005. One line shows China's car production, and the other shows India's.

# TAMING TRAFFIC

As the number of cars on the road grows, the number of accidents often grows, too. More car use also means more traffic. Traffic jams are a part of life in many large cities.

As traffic gets worse, many cities are looking for ways to get cars off the road. People must pay a fee to drive in central London during peak hours. In Seattle, Washington, USA, people can ride buses in the centre of town for free.

Sharing cars has become popular in many cities. People can reserve the use of a car for a few hours or a few days. A study of this program in Germany and Belgium showed that people who give up their own cars and use shared cars drive considerably less.

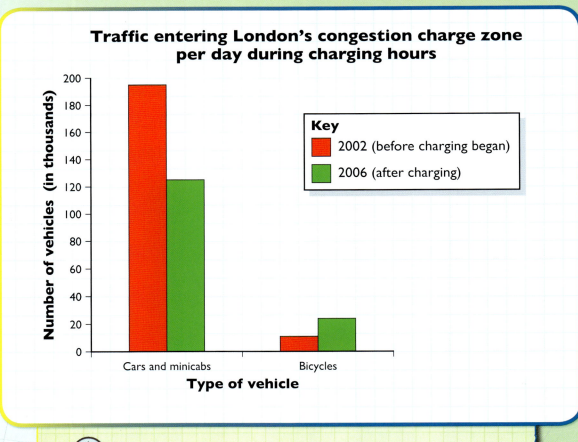

**Traffic entering London's congestion charge zone per day during charging hours**

Number of vehicles (in thousands)

Key
2002 (before charging began)
2006 (after charging)

Type of vehicle

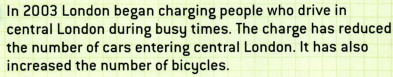

In 2003 London began charging people who drive in central London during busy times. The charge has reduced the number of cars entering central London. It has also increased the number of bicycles.

# Boosting bike use

Some places encourage people to ride bicycles instead of drive. But cycling on roads shared with cars can be dangerous. Some places have bike lanes on the sides of their streets. Others have special cycle lanes where no cars are allowed.

Many cities are also starting bicycle share programs. People in Paris can borrow and return bicycles from one of over 1,000 stations throughout the city. They can use the bikes for free for 30 minutes.

## Time and fuel

Traffic wastes time, and it also wastes **fuel**. A study of traffic in United States cities showed traffic delays around Los Angeles, California cost drivers 72 hours a year. The delays also waste 215 litres of fuel per driver each year.

 Cycle lanes make cycling safer and more appealing.

# TRAVELLING TOGETHER

**Public transport** helps to reduce car use. When people ride together on trains, underground systems, ferries, or buses, they help keep cars off the street. A bus may carry 50 passengers. If all 50 of those people drove cars instead, traffic would be worse.

Although public transport saves **fuel** and improves traffic, it is not practical in all places. It makes the most sense in cities, where many people live in a relatively small area.

## Buses

A bus can carry many more people than a car can. Most buses travel along regular routes. They stop at bus stops to pick up customers. Some buses run on diesel fuel. Some run on natural gas, a fuel that makes less **pollution** than diesel. Others run on electricity. They move along overhead electric cables that stretch the length of the bus route. The buses attach to the cables to get the power.

 Two ferries carry passengers in Hong Kong.

# Trains

Some trains run underground. They do not need to compete with car traffic or slow down for people crossing the street. The world's first underground railway opened in London in 1863. Today there are underground systems in cities all around the world.

Some trains that carry people to work run on ordinary railway tracks. They may share the tracks with freight trains. Other trains, called elevated trains, run on tracks above city streets. They avoid street traffic, as underground trains do. In the Philippines, much of Manila's Metro Rail Transit runs on elevated tracks.

## Along the cables

Cable cars in San Francisco, USA, carry tourists and local people up and down the city's steep hills. An underground cable pulls the cars, which weigh about 6 tonnes, along.

 Los Angeles is much larger and more spread out than New York. Can you see how this affects the way people travel?

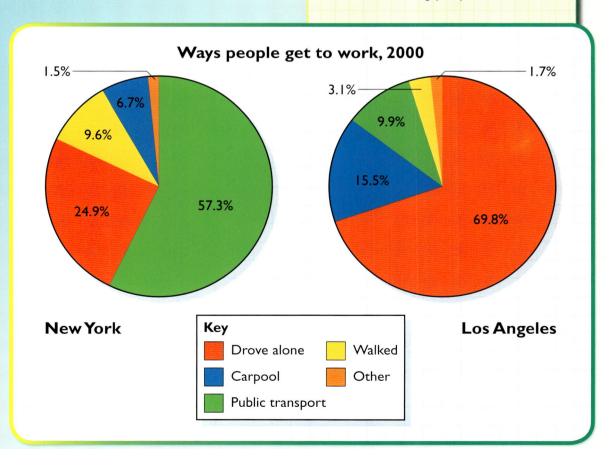

**Ways people get to work, 2000**

New York:
- 1.5%
- 6.7%
- 9.6%
- 24.9%
- 57.3%

Los Angeles:
- 3.1%
- 1.7%
- 9.9%
- 15.5%
- 69.8%

**New York**

**Los Angeles**

**Key**
- Drove alone
- Carpool
- Public transport
- Walked
- Other

The use of motor vehicles creates **pollution**. Most cars are powered by petrol or diesel **fuel**. When these fuels are burned, they release **emissions** into the air. These include small particles and gases such as carbon dioxide. More gas-burning cars means more pollution.

## Global warming

Carbon dioxide is a **greenhouse gas**. The Earth is surrounded by a blanket of gases called the **atmosphere**. Carbon dioxide and other gases in the atmosphere trap the sun's heat and keep the Earth warm.

But if there are too many greenhouse gases in the air, they trap too much heat. The temperature of the Earth starts to slowly rise. This is called **global warming**.

Scientists believe the planet is warming up because of greenhouse gases humans make. If this warming is not stopped, it will cause many problems. Ice in the Arctic has started to melt, affecting the animals that live there. As ice melts, the sea level may rise and cause flooding. Even a small **climate** change can have a big effect on animals and plants.

 Pollution hangs in the air above Mexico City, Mexico.

## Oil running out

Petrol and diesel are made from oil. Oil is a **fossil fuel**. Fossil fuels are made from dead animals and plants. They take millions of years to form. The Earth has a limited supply of them. Fossil fuels are non-renewable resources. If we run out, the Earth will not make more of them for a long time.

## Petrol pollution

A bar chart may use bars of different colours to show different **data**. This triple bar chart shows the carbon dioxide emissions caused by **petroleum** use. It gives data for a number of countries. For each country, one colour bar shows the emissions in 1985, another colour shows 1995, and a third colour shows 2005.

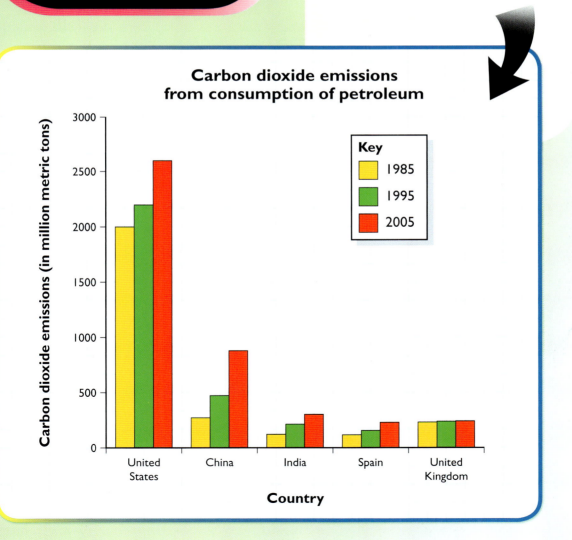

**Carbon dioxide emissions from consumption of petroleum**

Key
- 1985
- 1995
- 2005

Carbon dioxide emissions (in million metric tons)

Country: United States, China, India, Spain, United Kingdom

The way we power our vehicles needs to change. The Earth has a limited supply of **fossil fuels**. **Global warming** and **pollution** are harming the environment. Changing the **fuels** we use in vehicles can help solve these problems.

**Ethanol** can be made from plants such as sugar cane and corn. It is a renewable resource. Ethanol can be used alone or mixed with petrol. In 2007, over 85 percent of cars sold in Brazil were flex-fuel cars, which can run on either petrol or ethanol. Flex-fuel cars are not a new idea. The Model T Ford, made 100 years ago, was a flex-fuel car!

**Biodiesel** gives off fewer **emissions** than standard diesel fuel. It is a renewable resource made from vegetable oil. Biodiesel can even be made from the used vegetable oil fast-food restaurants use for frying!

**US biodiesel production**

1 US gallon = 3.785 litres

US biodiesel production (millions of gallons) vs Year

 This graph shows the increasing amount of biodiesel made in the United States.

 Electric cars run more cleanly than cars powered by petrol. To recharge a car, the owner plugs it into an electrical outlet.

# Electric cars and hybrids

Electric cars run on electricity stored in rechargeable batteries. The cars themselves do not release emissions. However, power plants make electricity that charges the cars' batteries. If the power plants run on fossil fuels, they contribute to global warming.

Hybrid cars are powered by both petrol and electricity. They get better mileage than cars that run only on petrol, and they make less pollution. Hybrids have become popular in the United States, Japan, and the United Kingdom.

## A green solution?

Fuel cells mix hydrogen with oxygen from the air to make heat and electricity. Instead of harmful emissions, fuel cells give off water as a waste product. There are currently problems with fuel cells – for example, they are expensive. But someday, cars may be powered by fuel cells instead of petrol.

In 1961, a Russian astronaut named Yuri Gagarin became the first person to fly into space. Since then, humans have travelled far from the Earth. People have walked on the moon. Most years there are several space flights that carry humans. Space probes, which do not have humans aboard, also collect information and send it back to Earth.

 A timeline puts events in order and shows how much time passed between events. This timeline shows some important events in the space program.

## The space shuttle

The space shuttle carries people into space. One of the shuttle's jobs is to take people and supplies to the International Space Station. The space station is a research lab being built in the skies above the Earth.

When the shuttle takes off, most of the launch power comes from two solid rocket boosters. Shortly after take-off, the boosters drop into the ocean, and boats carry them back to land. A **fuel** tank also separates from the shuttle when it is empty. The tank falls towards the Earth and breaks up in the Earth's **atmosphere**.

### Events in the space program

| | |
|---|---|
| 1960 | **1961**: First human travels into space |
| 1965 | |
| 1970 | **1969**: Humans land on the moon |
| 1975 | |
| | **1976**: Viking spacecraft lands on Mars (no humans aboard) |
| 1980 | **1981**: First space shuttle flight |
| 1985 | **1983**: Pioneer 10 spacecraft becomes first space probe to leave solar system (no humans aboard) |
| 1990 | **1990**: Hubble Space Telescope launched into orbit around Earth |
| 1995 | |
| | **1998**: Construction begins on International Space Station |
| 2000 | |
| 2005 | **2004**: Cassini-Huygens becomes first space probe to orbit Saturn (no humans aboard) |

A shuttle carrying **cargo** into space seems very different from a child carrying newspapers on their bike. But space shuttles and bikes are both types of **transportation**, just like cars, boats, and trains. Different types of transportation let people travel and move things around. They help us explore the Earth – and other worlds far off in space.

 This photograph shows the space shuttle, its rocket boosters, and its huge orange fuel tank.

## Breaking free

Vehicles that travel into space must be powerful enough to break free of the Earth's **gravity**. Gravity is the strong force that keeps you from floating in the air, and pulls a ball you throw to the ground. Breaking free of gravity requires a large amount of energy.

Data is information about something. We often get important data as a mass of numbers, and it is difficult to make any sense of them. Graphs and charts are ways of displaying information visually. This helps us to see relationships and patterns in the data. Different types of graphs or charts are good for displaying different types of information.

## Pie charts

A pie chart is used to show the different parts of a whole picture. A pie chart is the best way to show how something is divided up. These charts show information as different sized portions of a circle. They can help you compare proportions. You can easily see which section is the largest slice of the pie.

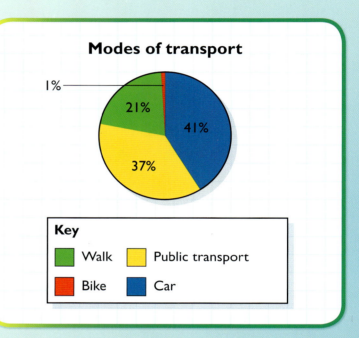

**Modes of transport**

1%
21%
41%
37%

**Key**

- ▇ Walk
- ▇ Public transport
- ▇ Bike
- ▇ Car

## Bar charts

Bar charts are a good way to compare amounts of different things. Bar charts have a vertical **y-axis** showing the **scale**, and a horizontal **x-axis** showing the different types of information. Bars of different colours can show different sets of data on the same graph.

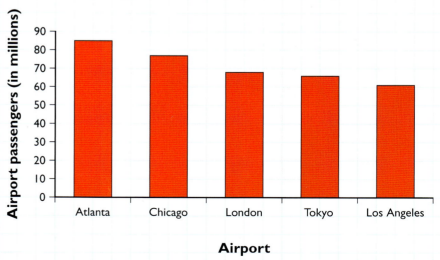

**Passenger traffic in top world airports, 2006**

Airport passengers (in millions)

90
80
70
60
50
40
30
20
10
0

Atlanta   Chicago   London   Tokyo   Los Angeles

**Airport**

# Pictograms

A pictogram uses pictures to show data.

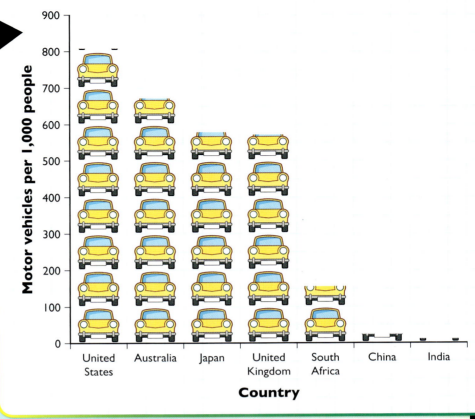

**Number of motor vehicles around the world, 2005**

Motor vehicles per 1,000 people — Country: United States, Australia, Japan, United Kingdom, South Africa, China, India

# Line graphs

Line graphs use lines to join up points on a graph. They can be used to show how something changes over time. If you put several lines on one line graph, you can compare the overall pattern of several sets of data. Time periods, such as months, are usually shown on the x-axis.

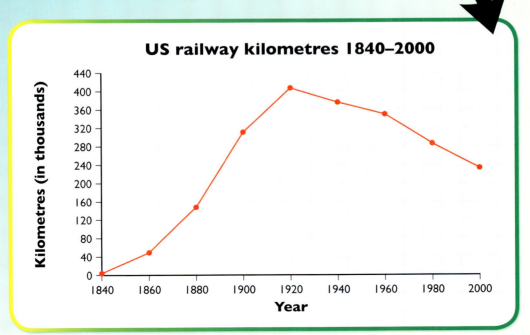

**US railway kilometres 1840–2000**

Kilometres (in thousands) — Year

# GLOSSARY

**atmosphere** layer of gases around the Earth

**biodiesel** fuel made from vegetable oil

**cargo** goods carried by a vehicle such as a ship or lorry

**climate** the general type of weather an area has, over a period of time

**data** information, often in the form of numbers

**domestic freight** cargo carried inside one country

**emissions** something put into the air

**ethanol** fuel made from plants such as corn or sugar cane

**fossil fuel** fuel such as coal, oil, or natural gas made from animals and plants that lived millions of years ago

**fuel** something that provides energy; for instance, the fuel petrol provides energy for some engines

**global warming** increase in the Earth's temperature

**goods** things to be bought or sold

**gravity** force that pulls things towards the Earth

**greenhouse gas** carbon dioxide or other gas that traps heat in the atmosphere

**key** something that shows what the symbols or colours on a graph mean

**maglev** type of train moved by powerful magnets

**petroleum** oil used to make petrol

**pollution** harmful substances put into the air, water, or soil

**public transport** buses, underground systems, or other types of transportation that carry many passengers

**scale** relationship between the marks on a graph's axis and the measurement the graph is showing (for example, one mark on the y-axis might represent 1,000 kilometres)

**transportation** way of carrying people or products from one place to another

**x-axis** horizontal line on a graph

**y-axis** vertical line on a graph

# FURTHER INFORMATION

## Books

*Eyewitness: Train*, John Coiley (DK Publishing, 2000)

*Go!*, Samone Bos, Phil Hunt, and Andrea Mills (DK Publishing, 2006)

*I Wonder Why Planes Have Wings and Other Questions About Transportation*, Christopher Maynard (Kingfisher, 2003)

## Websites

The American website for the National Centre for Educational Statistics has a section where you can create different types of graphs and charts.
http://nces.ed.gov/nceskids/createagraph/

The EcoFriendly Kids website regularly updates its articles showing how families can live in a way that has less impact on the environment, including this section on travel and transport.
www.ecofriendlykids.co.uk/TravellingCategory.html

The American Energy Information Administration's energy kid's page has lots of facts, fun activities, and games about energy.
www.eia.doe.gov/kids/energyfacts/index.html

The Climate Change kid's website gives many examples of small changes young people can make in their everyday lives to help the planet.
www.epa.gov/climatechange/kids/difference.html

Exploratorium's Science of Cycling website tells you all about the physics and forces behind cycling, how gears help you go uphill, and how cycling has changed over the years. There are clips of famous racing cyclists and even music from a band that tours by bike!
www.exploratorium.edu/cycling/

# INDEX